M000168733

Book 2
Grades K–2

Lollipop Logic

**Bonnie Risby
& Robert K. Risby, II**

**Illustrated by
Joshua Krezinski**

PRUFROCK PRESS INC.
WACO, TEXAS

Edited by Sarah Morrison

Cover Design by Raquel Trevino

ISBN-13: 978-1-59363-713-2

Printed in the United States of America.

At the time of this book's publication, all facts and figures cited are the most current available. All telephone numbers, addresses, and website URLs are accurate and active. All publications, organizations, websites, and other resources exist as described in the book, and all have been verified. The authors and Prufrock Press Inc. make no warranty or guarantee concerning the information and materials given out by organizations or content found at websites, and we are not responsible for any changes that occur after this book's publication. If you find an error, please contact Prufrock Press Inc.

Prufrock Press Inc.
P.O. Box 8813
Waco, TX 76714-8813
Phone: (800) 998-2208
Fax: (800) 240-0333
http://www.prufrock.com

Table of Contents

Lollipop Logic (Book 2)

Lesson	Common Core State Standards
Sequences (Lessons 1-8)	**Math:** K.CC.A Know number names and the count sequence.
Relationships (Lessons 9-16)	**ELA-Literacy:** L.K.5 With guidance and support from adults, explore word relationships and nuances in word meanings. L.1.5 With guidance and support from adults, demonstrate understanding of word relationships and nuances in word meanings
Analogies (Lessons 17-24)	**Math:** K.G.B Analyze, compare, create, and compose shapes. 1.G.A & 2.G.A Reason with shapes and their attributes. **ELA-Literacy:** L.K.5 With guidance and support from adults, explore word relationships and nuances in word meanings. L.1.5 With guidance and support from adults, demonstrate understanding of word relationships and nuances in word meanings
Deduction (Lessons 25-31)	**ELA/Literacy:** RF.K.1 & R.F.1.1 Demonstrate understanding of the organization and basic features of print. RF.K.3, R.F.1.3, & R.F.2.3 Know and apply grade-level phonics and word analysis skills in decoding words. R.F.1.4 & R.F.2.4 Read with sufficient accuracy and fluency to support comprehension.
Pattern Decoding (Lessons 32-39)	**Math:** 4.OA.C Generate and analyze patterns.
Critical Analysis (Lessons 50-52)	**Math:** K.CC.B Count to tell the number of objects. K.CC.C. Compare numbers. K.G.B Analyze, compare, create, and compose shapes. 1.G.A & 2.G.A Reason with shapes and their attributes.

Notes:

1. The standard addressed by the Pattern Decoding section of Lollipop Logic, Book 2, is listed as a fourth-grade Operations and Algebra standard by the CCSS. Although the concept of patterns may be addressed at a lower grade level, as it is in the activities in this section, the standard in this sheet reflects the first time it is covered in the CCSS.

2. Although the book was designed with the prereader in mind, the Deduction section includes clues and instructions that an early or emerging reader could read on his or her own to solve the activities, thus meeting the standards for Reading Foundations.

About This Book

Lollipop Logic is designed to present critical thinking skills to young students who may not yet have mastered reading skills. In the past, these skills have been reserved for much older students; however, there is nothing lacking in the development of very young students to prohibit introducing and nurturing these skills other than a degree of reading proficiency. *Lollipop Logic* is unique in that it combines problems involving deduction, analogies, relationships, sequencing, pattern decoding, inference, and critical analyzing skills in a format designed to appeal to students in grades K–2—without any reading barrier. As young children develop these thinking skills, expect to see them approach all materials with critical forethought.

To the Teacher

Lollipop Logic is the direct result of requests by educators for lessons presenting critical thinking skills in a format suitable for younger students. The teacher is indeed the most important element in making critical thinking skills work for younger students. It is the instructor's role not only to present the process, but also to foster an atmosphere where creative and critical thinking are encouraged and any fear of failure is absent. Because the thought process itself is more important than the answers provided in the back of the book, it is very important to discuss and compare methods that students use to arrive at conclusions and to be tolerant of creative diversions from the norm. It is suggested that each new type of skill be presented and discussed and that sample problems be worked together before students are challenged to work independently.

Skills Presented in This Book

Sequences. Sequencing problems require students to look at time relationships. Pictorial sequences presented here require young thinkers to look at a group of illustrations to determine the relationship before selecting the item that must come first, the one coming second, and so forth. They must study the illustrations to discover the relationship that dictates the sequence. They should always be encouraged to take care to correct any error that would create subsequent errors in the sequencing pattern.

Relationships. In this section, students will be looking for ways that certain things relate to one another. Some of the relationships will be obvious;

others will be more subtle. Students should be reminded to be flexible and creative and not to become alarmed when the relationship they define is different than one discovered by their neighbors. Exercises in this section should be completed before introducing analogies, as analogical thinking is based on being able to identify relationships.

Analogies. Analogies are comparisons between things based on similar characteristics. This section contains both figural and pictorial analogies that are very similar to the literal or verbal analogies undertaken by older students. Although first attempts may be awkward, young children usually catch on to analogies quite readily, find them challenging, and relate to them with the adventurousness of one learning a new sport. To solve the analogies, students must find the relationship between the first two items and then establish the same or a very similar relationship between a second pair of items that completes the analogy. It would be helpful to go through several examples together before beginning individual work.

Deduction. Deduction is a form of inference in which the conclusion follows from premises or statements of fact. Because we are targeting a non-reading population, we have endeavored to keep the clues extremely brief. Teachers should read the clues clearly, repeat them carefully, and then allow the learner adequate time to solve the problem by logically linking together all of the facts.

Pattern Decoding. Exercises in pattern decoding present a series of figures that represent a pattern. Students are to study the illustrations to discover the pattern. Once they have discovered the pattern, they are to select one other illustration that would come next in the pattern. There are several skills that come into play in these exercises. Students must be able to distinguish between the visual images, recognize the pattern that is presented, and forecast what the next element in the sequence will be. If students encounter trouble in completing the pattern, it may be necessary to go back and review one or more aspects of this skill.

Inference. The use of inference is a broad area of logic. Inference involves reaching conclusions from gathered evidence. It means going from the known to the unknown and forming educated guesses based on either facts or premises. This book includes pictorial exercises to introduce students to inference-based thinking. They must critically examine the pictorial evidence presented and proceed to the next logical step or to the conclusion that is required.

Critical Analysis. Critical analyzing skills involve examining given information and reaching conclusions from gathered evidence. This process is very similar to one of the oldest logic arguments, syllogisms. The young thinkers are presented with two groups of items, represented entirely with pictures, to carefully scrutinize and analyze. They know the following:

- All members of group A are Z.
- All members of group B are not Z.

Then they are presented with new items to examine and determine whether or not they are Z. The pictures in both groups are nonsensical. They do, however, establish valid relationships that will lead to and support conclusions.

Teacher's Instructions

Sequences (Lessons 1–8)

Note: For all sequencing lessons, caution students against marking the blanks too quickly without careful consideration. Remind them that an error in an early step of the solution could cause subsequent errors.

Lesson 1: Preface this exercise in sequencing by explaining that a spider is spinning its web. Each picture represents a logical step that must either precede or follow another sequential step. Explain that there is only one logically acceptable solution, so students must consider the order very carefully. Students should label the first step in the sequence "1," the second "2," and so on.

Lesson 2: Explain that the following pictures show sand passing through an hourglass. Ask students to carefully consider which picture comes first, and then place a "1" in the blank by that picture. They should place a "2" by the picture that comes second, and so forth. Be sure that students realize there is only one correct sequence.

Lesson 3: Preface this exercise in sequencing by explaining that a candle is about to be lit and then melt. Students will see six pictures representing the different stages of the candle melting. Explain that there is only one logically acceptable solution, so students must consider carefully the order of the pictures. Students should number the pictures in the order in which they will happen.

Lesson 4: Instruct the students that what they are about to see is six views of the same piggy bank. The piggy bank starts out empty, but by the end, its owner has lots of coins. By carefully considering the pictures, students can determine whether each of the six pictures precedes or follows another picture in the sequence. Explain that there is only one logically acceptable solution, so students must consider carefully the order of the pictures. Students should number the pictures in the order in which they will happen.

Lesson 5: Preface this exercise in sequencing by explaining that someone is blowing up a balloon. Students will see six pictures representing progressive stages of the balloon getting bigger—perhaps even escaping from the person blowing it up. Explain that there is only one logically acceptable solution, so they must consider carefully the order of the pictures. Students should number the pictures to show the order in which they will happen.

Lesson 6: Preface this exercise in sequencing by explaining that a seed has been planted in the soil. Students will see six pictures representing progressive stages from germination of the seed to its growth into a mature plant. Explain that there is only one logically acceptable solution, so students must consider carefully the order of the pictures. Students should number the pictures in the order they think they will happen.

Lesson 7: Preface this exercise in sequencing by explaining that someone is performing on the high dive. The pictures students are about to see will represent the progressive stages of the diver reaching the platform and leaping into a pool. Explain that there is only one logically acceptable solution, so students must consider carefully the order of the pictures. Students should number the pictures according to the order in which they will happen.

Lesson 8: Explain to students that they are going to see several pictures showing a pizza being eaten. Explain that there is only one logically acceptable solution, so students must consider carefully the order of the pictures. Students should number the pictures according to the order in which they will happen.

Relationships (Lessons 9–16)

Lessons 9–12: All of the lessons in this section have the same instructions. Read the following instructions to students.

Look at the first thing in the row, the thing that is in the small box. It has something in common with one of the three things in the big box next to it. It could be that they are the same shape, the same design, the same size, or are alike in some other way. Find the picture that is most like the first picture and draw a circle around it.

Lessons 13–16: All of the lessons in this section have the same instructions. Read the following instructions to students.

A group of things that belong together are in the box. Look at the items in this group carefully to determine what they have in common or why they belong together. Then look carefully at the items below the box and decide if they could belong with the items in the boxed group. If they *do* belong to the group of things in the box, draw a circle around them. If they *do not* belong to the group, draw an X through them.

Analogies (Lessons 17–24)

Analogies are comparisons between two sets of things. They compare features that are not always obvious. Approach these pictorial and figural analogies with very young learners by carefully examining and talking about the examples given. Remember, this is a completely new concept for these young individuals. Don't be discouraged by awkward first attempts. Also, remember that it is the process itself that we want to instill, so working in groups and sharing with the class are good initial approaches.

Lessons 17–19: For each of these lessons, read the following instructions to students.

Look at the two things in the first box. Think about how they are related. Then look at the picture to the right of the box. One of the three choices is related to this thing in the same way the first two things are related. Find the one thing that is related to the third thing in the same way the first two things are related. Draw a circle around this thing.

Lessons 20–24: For all of these lessons, read the following instructions to students.

Look at the first two pictures. Think about how they are related. Then look for the two pictures underneath the top two pictures that are related to each other in the same way. Circle the correct pair.

Deduction (Lessons 25–31)

The activities in this section are designed with the prereader in mind; however, listening comprehension is required. Also, the student must be able to distinguish the four characters in the activity. The figures are labeled, but some learners may wish to color the characters or code them in some other manner. Read the problem and clues slowly and distinctly, pause to allow thinking, and reread clues. This presentation can be repeated as many times as necessary. If students are working in pairs or small groups, allow them enough time to discuss their solutions. Have students draw a line from each character to the item with which that character is associated.

Lesson 25: Chopsticks and Fortune Cookies

Sebastian, Evan, Emma, and Falon all ordered takeout from a Chinese menu. They ordered Sesame Chicken, Shrimp Fried Rice, Pork Egg Foo Young, and General Tso's Beef. Listen carefully to the clues, and then draw a line connecting each person with what he or she bought.

Clues

1. Emma and the girl ordering Shrimp Fried Rice both had cookies containing identical fortunes.
2. Evan and his friend Sebastian ordered chicken and pork and were very excited to try using chopsticks.
3. Evan did **not** order the Pork Egg Foo Young.

Lesson 26: Prism Crayon Company

Sydney, Lydia, Rob, and Tyler all participated in a poll sponsored by the Prism Crayon Company. Each child was asked to use the new colors from the company, and then to pick his or her two favorites. The color pairs chosen were hummingbird green / red velvet, watermelon pink / robin's-egg blue, mulberry purple / jack-o-lantern orange, and swallowtail yellow / cedar green. Listen carefully to the clues, and then draw a line connecting each person with the color that he or she picked.

Clues

1. Rob and Sydney both had a shade of green in their pair of favorite colors.
2. Tyler and the girl choosing watermelon pink had a hard time choosing only two colors.
3. Sydney did **not** choose red velvet.

Lesson 27: Hiking Snacks

Crystal, Julie, Nick, and Clayton all hiked the Chipmunk Trail at White Oak Park. Halfway through the hike, they took a break to share their snacks: string cheese, apple slices, juice pouches, and strawberry leather. Listen carefully to the clues, and then draw a line connecting each person with the snack he or she carried in a backpack.

Clues

1. Nick and the boy who brought juice to share were glad to empty their backpacks.
2. Crystal and the girl sharing apple slices also brought wipes and napkins to share.
3. Nick did **not** bring the strawberry leather.

Lesson 28: Vacation on the Coast

Grandma Tonia, Grandpa Dave, Becky, and Sebastian took a vacation to the Georgia Coast. Their stay was very enjoyable, and each person had a favorite memory: collecting shells at low tide, visiting the turtle sanctuary, identifying birds in the salt marshes, and bumping into former President Bill Clinton at a seafood restaurant. Listen carefully to the clues, and then draw a line connecting each person with his or her favorite vacation memory.

Clues

1. Sebastian and his mom visited the beach at low tide and also visited the turtle sanctuary.
2. Grandma Tonia loved sitting on the balcony early in the morning, when the birds became active in the marshes.
3. Becky is **not** the person whose favorite memory was the turtle sanctuary.

Lesson 29: The Birthday Album

Dakota, Taylor, Logan, and Jackson are making a combined birthday album-scrapbook. Each friend contributes photos and mementos from his or her birthday, held at one of the following places: the Water Park, the Bouncing Air Arcade, the Magic Park, and the Victorian Doll Museum. Listen carefully to the clues, and then draw a line connecting each person to his or her birthday celebration.

Clues

1. Dakota and the girl who celebrated at the quaint tearoom and the adjoining Victorian Doll Museum invited both boys and girls to their parties.
2. Jackson and the boy who loved bouncing at the Air Arcade both celebrate birthdays during the same month.
3. Dakota is **not** the person who celebrated at the Magic Park.

Lesson 30: Lavender Farm

Chloe, Kaitlyn, Aidan, and Landon visit the Lavender Farm. They all spend a wonderful afternoon there. Each person leaves with a different favorite memory: gathering bundles of lavender, sampling lavender lemonade and jelly, crafting lavender wreaths, and making lavender cookies. Listen carefully to the clues, and then draw a line connecting each person with his or her favorite Lavender Farm memory.

Clues

1. Chloe and the girl who spent most of her time gathering lavender planned to make sachets for gifts.
2. Aidan and the boy who enjoyed the lavender lemonade and jelly were amazed at how gentle the honeybees were that worked in

the lavender fields among the people gathering the wonderful-smelling stems.
3. Chloe is **not** the one who enjoyed making lavender cookies.

Lesson 31: County Fair

Shannon, Tasha, Colby, and Adam attend the county fair near their homes. While wandering the fairgrounds, they each have a different favorite activity: fishing for prizes, going down the giant slide, eating funnel cake, and putting golf balls at a target. Listen carefully to the clues, and then draw a line connecting each person to his or her favorite county fair activity.

Clues

1. Colby and the boy who could putt golf balls through a narrow opening stayed for the evening fireworks.
2. Shannon and the girl who loved fishing for plastic fish to win prizes had 25 tickets each.
3. Colby did **not** like funnel cake.

Pattern Decoding (Lessons 32–39)

All of the lessons in this section have the same instructions. Read the following instructions to the students. (Note that some items in the answer list may be used more than once, and some may not be used at all.)

Study the following patterns carefully. After you find the pattern, choose the item from the answer list that should come next. Draw a line connecting the pattern to the item in the list that should come next.

Inference (Lessons 40–49)

Lessons 40–41

Read the following instructions to students.

Each of the pictures below has a part that is missing. The missing parts are shown along the side of the page. Find the missing part of each picture. Draw a line between the picture and its missing section.

Lessons 42–43

Read the following instructions to students.

Each picture has a missing piece. Beside it are several pieces that could fit in the place of the missing piece. Only one piece will fit to correctly complete the picture. Choose the correct missing piece. Draw a circle around it.

Lessons 44–45
Read the following instructions to students.

Below are some pieces to a puzzle. Some of the pieces are missing. By carefully examining the pieces below, you can get an idea of what the total picture is. After you know what the puzzle represents, draw the picture on a separate piece of paper.

Lessons 46–47
Read the following instructions to students.

The left side shows several different pictures. On the right side, there are more pictures. Each picture on the left side is related to a picture on the right side in some way. Draw a line between each picture on the left and the picture on the right that it is most related to or goes with best.

Lesson 48–49
Read the following instructions for all lessons.

There are four different drawings on this page. The drawings show only part of a larger drawing. Look at this part carefully and see if you can guess what the whole picture would look like. Describe what you think this is a picture of.

Critical Analysis (Lessons 50–52)

Lessons 50–52
Read the following instructions, selecting the figure name that corresponds to the lesson.

Several species of new life forms have been discovered on the planet Olympianus. See if you can identify them. The top row shows things that are leemoys / shootles / beltazoids. The next row shows things that are not leemoys / shootles / beltazoids. Look at the creatures on the bottom and decide whether they are leemoys / shootles / beltazoids or not. If they are, draw a circle around them. If they are not, draw an X through them. Look back at the examples as often as you like.

Number these pictures to show the correct order.

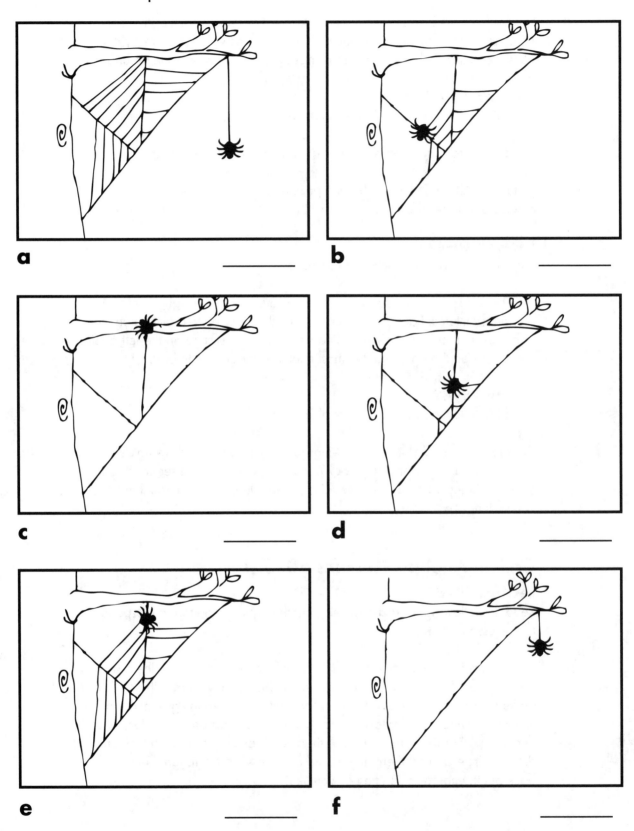

a _____

b _____

c _____

d _____

e _____

f _____

Number these pictures to show the correct order.

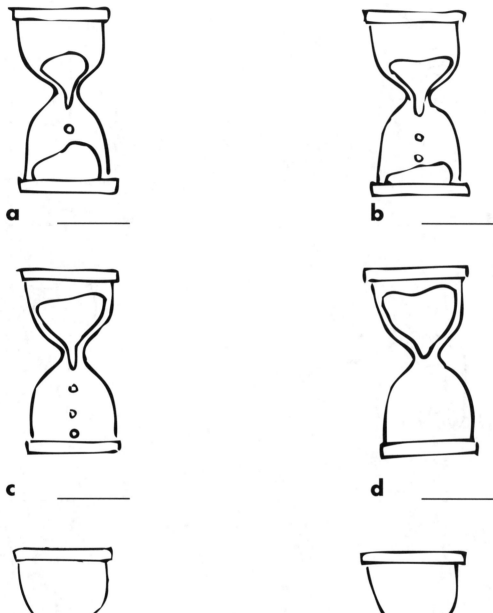

a _____

b _____

c _____

d _____

e _____

f _____

Number these pictures to show the correct order.

a _____

b _____

c _____

d _____

e _____

f _____

Lesson 4

Number these pictures to show the correct order.

a _____

b _____

c _____

d _____

e _____

f _____

Lesson 5

Number these pictures to show the correct order.

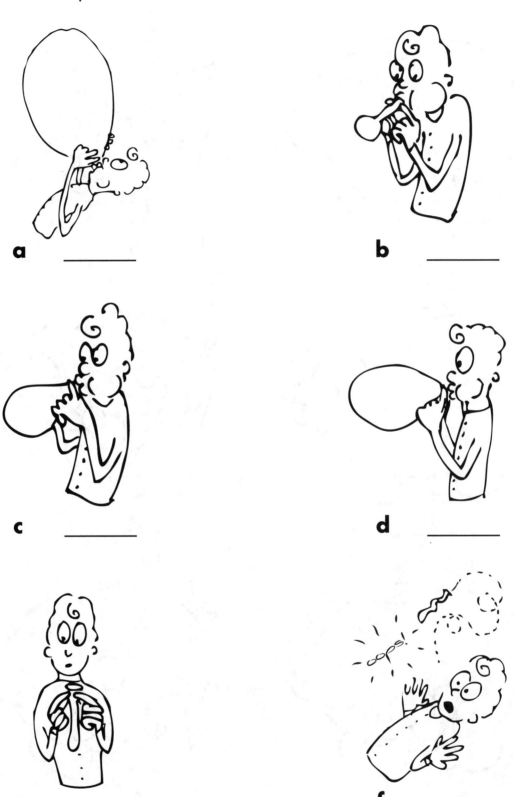

a _____

b _____

c _____

d _____

e _____

f _____

Number these pictures to show the correct order.

a _____

b _____

c _____

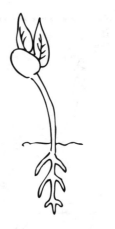

d _____

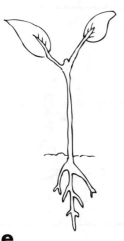

e _____

f _____

Number these pictures to show the correct order.

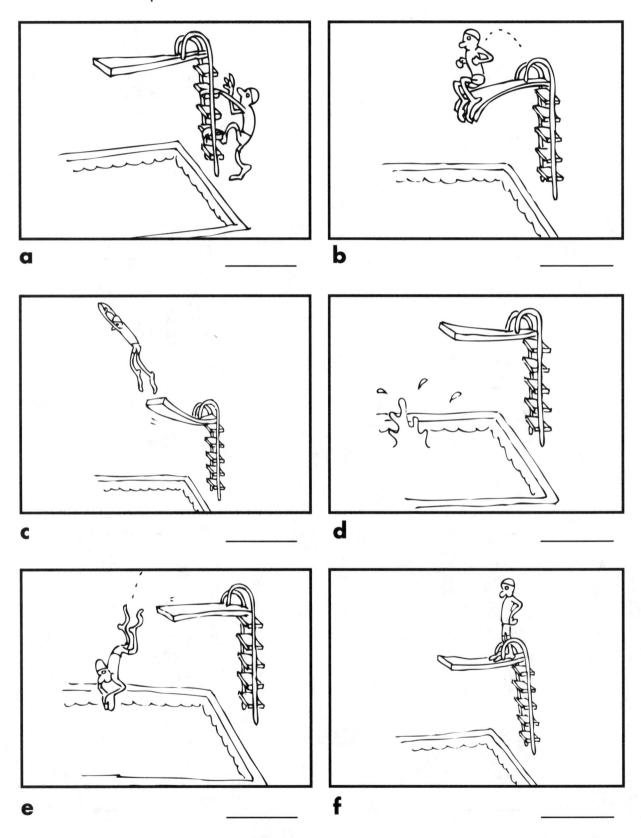

a _____

b _____

c _____

d _____

e _____

f _____

Number these pictures to show the correct order.

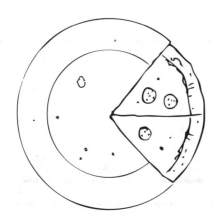

a _____

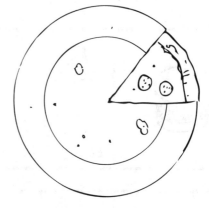

b _____

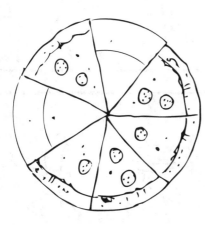

c _____

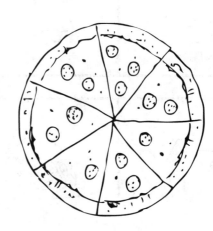

d _____

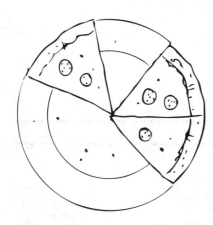

e _____

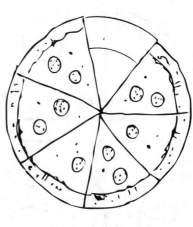

f _____

Lesson 9

Draw a circle around the picture that has something in common with the first picture.

Lesson 10

Draw a circle around the picture that has something in common with the first picture.

Lesson 11

Draw a circle around the picture that has something in common with the first picture.

Lesson 12

Draw a circle around the picture that has something in common with the first picture.

There is a group of related things in the box. Circle the things on this page that belong in the group. Put an X through the things that do not belong in the group.

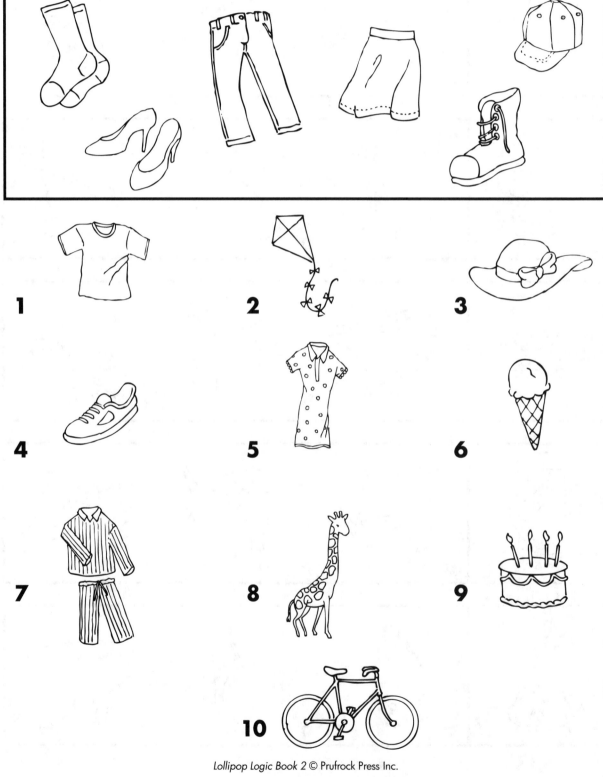

1

2

3

4

5

6

7

8

9

10

Lesson 14

There is a group of related things in the box. Circle the things on this page that belong in the group. Put an X through the things that do not belong in the group.

There is a group of related things in the box. Circle the things on this page that belong in the group. Put an X through the things that do not belong in the group.

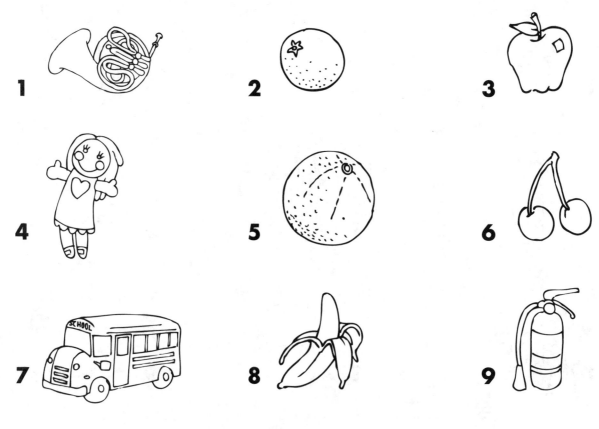

10

There is a group of related things in the box. Circle the things on this page that belong in the group. Put an X through the things that do not belong in the group.

Lesson 17

Circle the thing that is related to the third thing in the same way the first two things are related.

Lesson 18

Circle the thing that is related to the third thing in the same way the first two things are related.

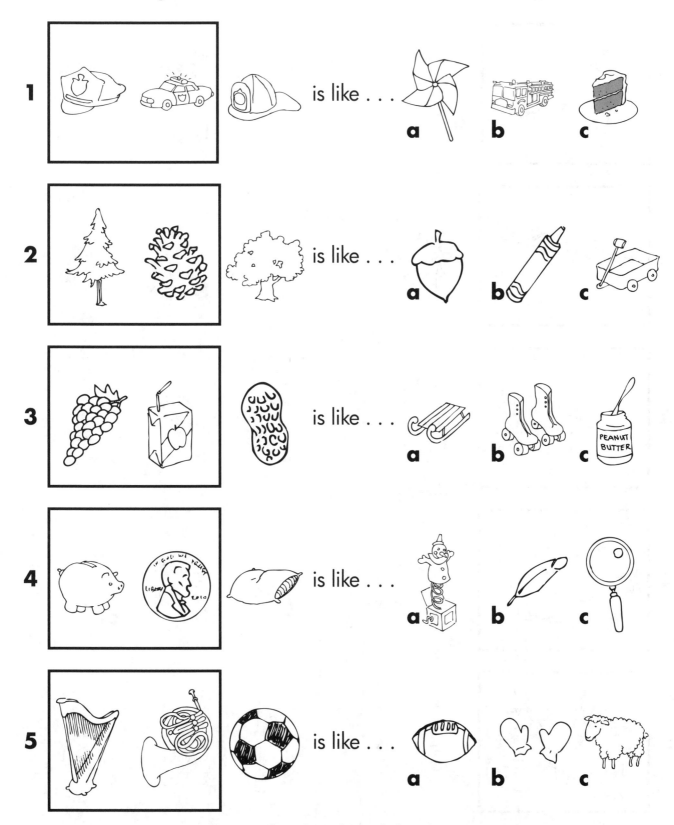

Lesson 19

Circle the thing that is related to the third thing in the same way the first two things are related.

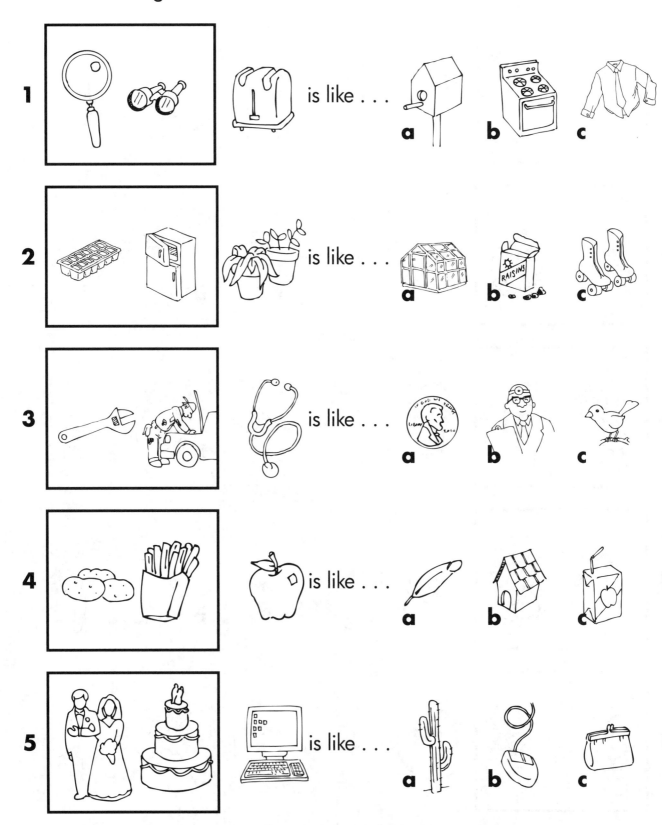

Lesson 20

Choose the pair of pictures that are related to each other in the same way the top two pictures are related. Circle the correct pair.

Example: is like as is like

1  is like ... as

a  is like ...

b 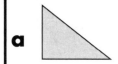 is like

c is like ...

2  is like as

a 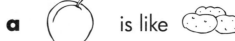 is like ...

b is like

c is like ...

3  is like ... as

a is like

b is like

c is like

4 is like as

a is like

b is like

c is like ...

Choose the pair of pictures that are related to each other in the same way the top two pictures are related. Circle the correct pair.

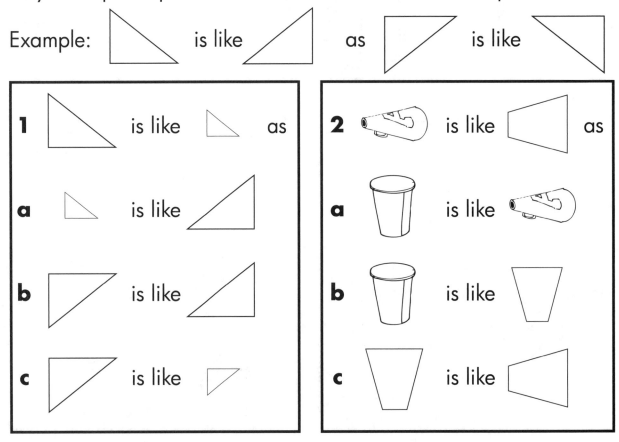

Example: ___ is like ___ as ___ is like ___

1 ___ is like ___ as

a ___ is like ___

b ___ is like ___

c ___ is like ___

2 ___ is like ___ as

a ___ is like ___

b ___ is like ___

c ___ is like ___

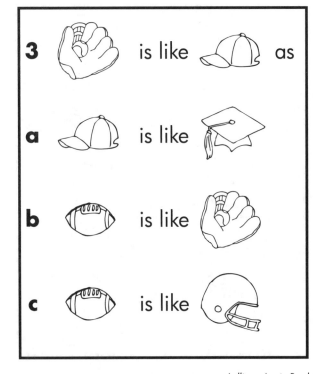

3 ___ is like ___ as

a ___ is like ___

b ___ is like ___

c ___ is like ___

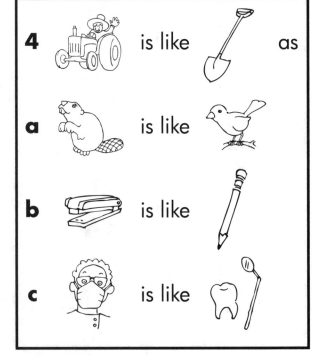

4 ___ is like ___ as

a ___ is like ___

b ___ is like ___

c ___ is like ___

Choose the pair of pictures that are related to each other in the same way the top two pictures are related. Circle the correct pair.

Example: ➡ is like ⬅ as ⬆ is like ⬇

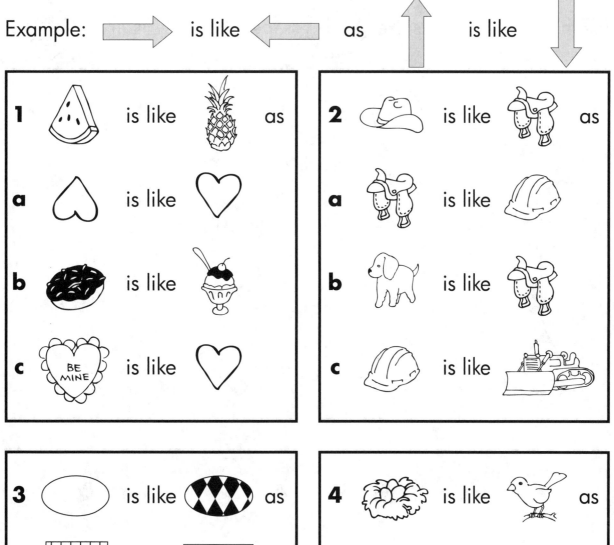

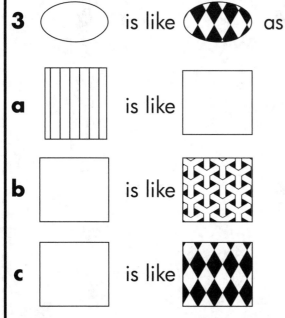

Lesson 23

Choose the pair of pictures that are related to each other in the same way the top two pictures are related. Circle the correct pair.

Example: [octagon] is like (STOP) as [diamond] is like (SCHOOL BUS STOP AHEAD)

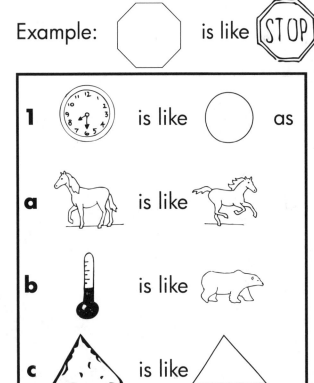

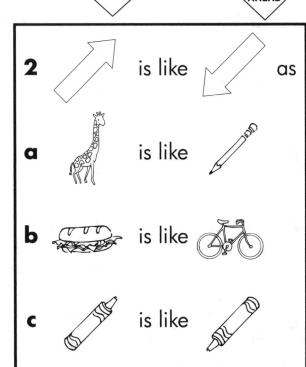

Choose the pair of pictures that are related to each other in the same way the top two pictures are related. Circle the correct pair.

Example: is like as is like

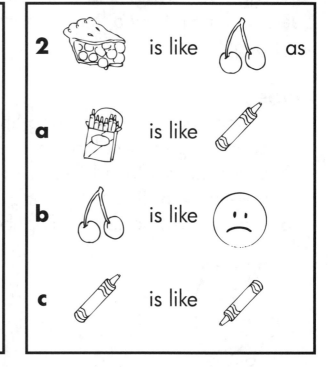

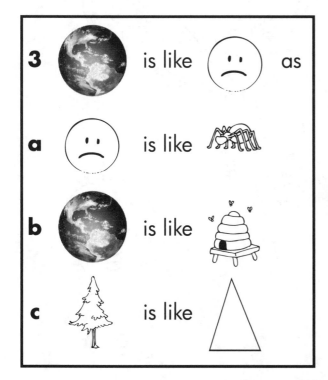

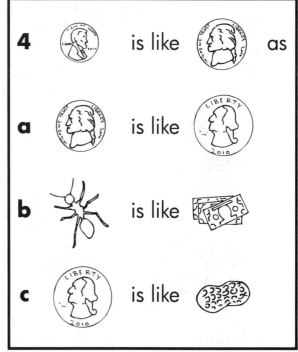

Chopsticks and Fortune Cookies

Sebastian, Evan, Emma, and Falon all ordered takeout from a Chinese menu. They ordered Sesame Chicken, Shrimp Fried Rice, Pork Egg Foo Young, and General Tso's Beef. Listen carefully to the clues, and then draw a line connecting each person with what he or she bought.

Clues

1. Emma and the girl ordering Shrimp Fried Rice both had cookies containing identical fortunes.
2. Evan and his friend Sebastian ordered chicken and pork and were very excited to try using chopsticks.
3. Evan did **not** order the Pork Egg Foo Young.

Sebastian

Evan

Falon

Emma

Prism Crayon Company

Sydney, Lydia, Rob, and Tyler all participated in a poll sponsored by the Prism Crayon Company. Each child was asked to use the new colors from the company, and then to pick his or her two favorites. The color pairs chosen were hummingbird green / red velvet, watermelon pink / robin's-egg blue, mulberry purple / jack-o-lantern orange, and swallowtail yellow / cedar green. Listen carefully to the clues, and then draw a line connecting each person with the two that he or she picked.

Clues

1. Rob and Sydney both had a shade of green in their pair of favorite colors.
2. Tyler and the girl choosing watermelon pink had a hard time choosing only two colors.
3. Sydney did **not** choose red velvet.

Hiking Snacks

Crystal, Julie, Nick, and Clayton all hiked the Chipmunk Trail at White Oak Park. Halfway through the hike, they took a break to share their snacks: string cheese, apple slices, juice pouches, and strawberry leather. Listen carefully to the clues, and then draw a line connecting each person with the snack he or she carried in a backpack.

Clues

1. Nick and the boy who brought juice to share were glad to empty their backpacks.
2. Crystal and the girl sharing apple slices also brought wipes and napkins to share.
3. Nick did **not** bring the strawberry leather.

Clayton

Nick

Crystal

Julie

Vacation on the Coast

Grandma Tonia, Grandpa Dave, Becky, and Sebastian took a vacation to the Georgia Coast. Their stay was very enjoyable, and each person had a favorite memory: collecting shells at low tide, visiting the turtle sanctuary, identifying birds in the salt marshes, and bumping into former President Bill Clinton at a seafood restaurant. Listen carefully to the clues, and then draw a line connecting each person with his or her favorite vacation memory.

Clues

1. Sebastian and his mom visited the beach at low tide and also visited the turtle sanctuary.
2. Grandma Tonia loved sitting on the balcony early in the morning, when the birds became active in the marshes.
3. Becky is **not** the person whose favorite memory was the turtle sanctuary.

Grandma Tonia

Grandpa Dave

Becky

Sebastian

The Birthday Album

Dakota, Taylor, Logan, and Jackson are making a combined birthday album-scrapbook. Each friend contributes photos and mementos from his or her birthday, held at one of the following places: the Water Park, the Bouncing Air Arcade, the Magic Park, and the Victorian Doll Museum. Listen carefully to the clues, and then draw a line connecting each person to his or her birthday celebration.

Clues

1. Dakota and the girl who celebrated at the quaint tearoom and the adjoining Victorian Doll Museum invited both boys and girls to their parties.
2. Jackson and the boy who loved bouncing at the Air Arcade both celebrate birthdays during the same month.
3. Dakota is **not** the person who celebrated at the Magic Park.

Jackson   Logan

Dakota   Taylor

Lavender Farm

Chloe, Kaitlyn, Aidan, and Landon visit the Lavender Farm. They all spend a wonderful afternoon there. Each person leaves with a different favorite memory: gathering bundles of lavender, sampling lavender lemonade and jelly, crafting lavender wreaths, and making lavender cookies. Listen carefully to the clues, and then draw a line connecting each person with his or her favorite Lavender Farm memory.

Clues

1. Chloe and the girl who spent most of her time gathering lavender planned to make sachets for gifts.
2. Aidan and the boy who enjoyed the lavender lemonade and jelly were amazed at how gentle the honeybees were that worked in the lavender fields among the people gathering the wonderful-smelling stems.
3. Chloe is **not** the one who enjoyed making lavender cookies.

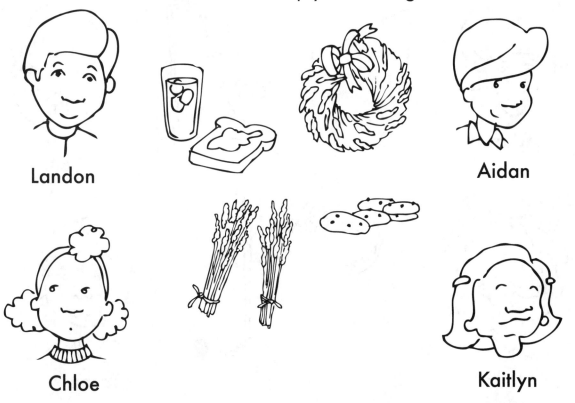

Landon   Aidan

Chloe   Kaitlyn

County Fair

Shannon, Tasha, Colby, and Adam attend the county fair near their homes. While wandering the fairgrounds, they each have a different favorite activity: fishing for prizes, going down the giant slide, eating funnel cake, and putting golf balls at a target. Listen carefully to the clues, and then draw a line connecting each person to his or her favorite county fair activity.

Clues

1. Colby and the boy who could putt golf balls through a narrow opening stayed for the evening fireworks.
2. Shannon and the girl who loved fishing for plastic fish to win prizes had 25 tickets each.
3. Colby did **not** like funnel cake.

Adam

Colby

Shannon

Tasha

Draw a line to the thing that should come next in each pattern.

1   **a**

2   **b**

3    **c**

4    **d**

5    **e**

Draw a line to the thing that should come next in each pattern.

1 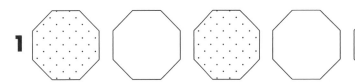   **a**

2 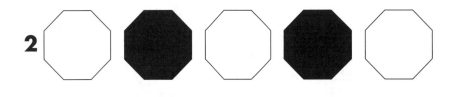   **b**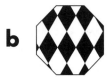

3 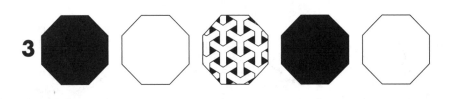   **c**

4 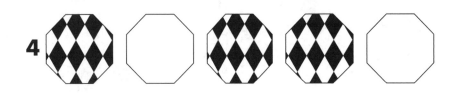   **d**

5 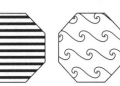   **e**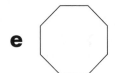

Draw a line to the thing that should come next in each pattern.

1    **a**

2 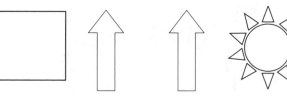   **b**

3  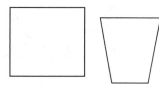   **c**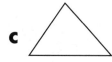

4 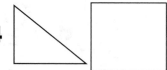 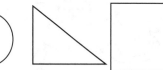   **d**

5     **e**

Draw a line to the thing that should come next in each pattern.

1      **a**

2       **b**

3      **c**

4        **d**

5   **e**

Draw a line to the thing that should come next in each pattern.

1    **a**

2    **b**

3    **c**

4    **d**

5    **e**

Draw a line to the thing that should come next in each pattern.

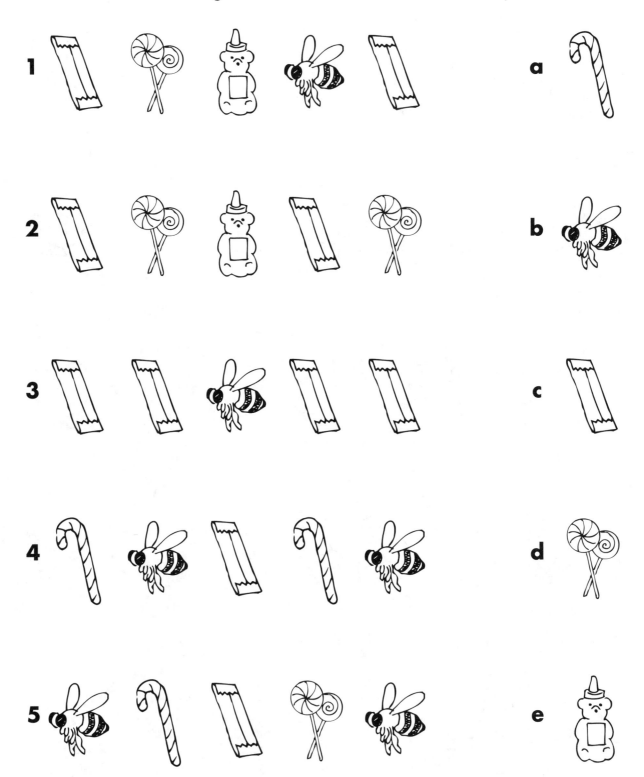

Draw a line to the thing that should come next in each pattern.

1    **a**

2    **b**

3    **c**

4    **d**

5    **e**

Draw a line to the thing that should come next in each pattern.

1    **a**

2    **b**

3 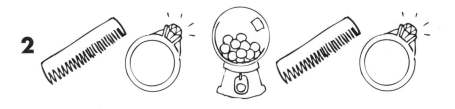   **c**

4    **d**

5    **e**

Draw a line between each picture and the piece that would fit with it to make a complete picture.

1

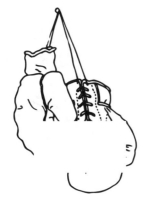

a

2

b

3

c

4

d

Draw a line between each picture and the piece that would fit with it to make a complete picture.

1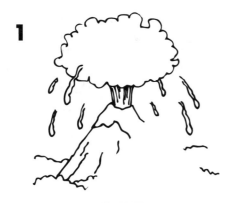

a

2

b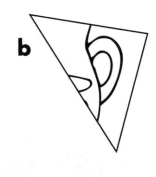

3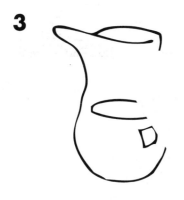

c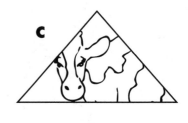

4

d

Find the correct missing piece to complete each picture. Draw a circle around it.

1

a   **b**   **c**

2

a 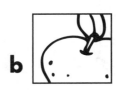   **b**    **c**

3

a    **b**    **c**

4

a   **b**   **c**

Find the correct missing piece to complete each picture. Draw a circle around it.

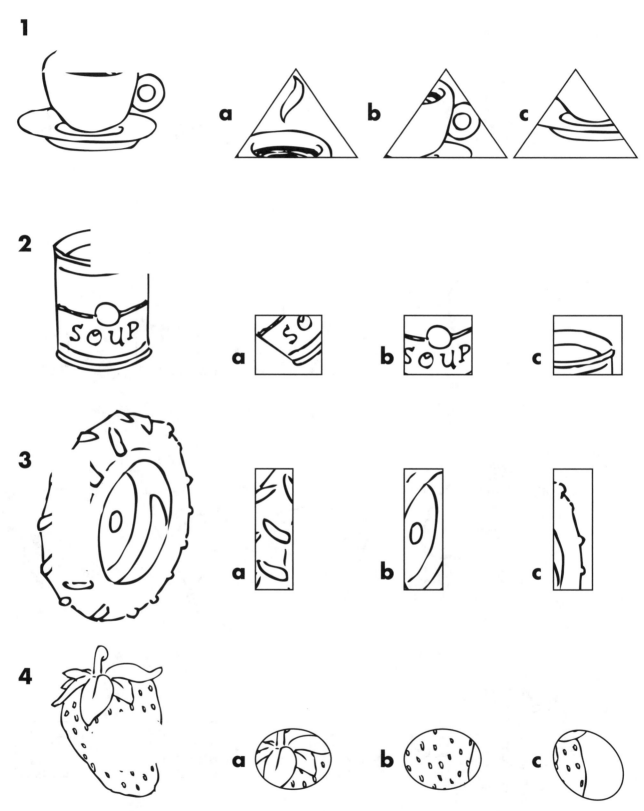

Lesson 44

Look at the puzzle pieces. Decide what picture is on the puzzle. Draw it on a separate piece of paper.

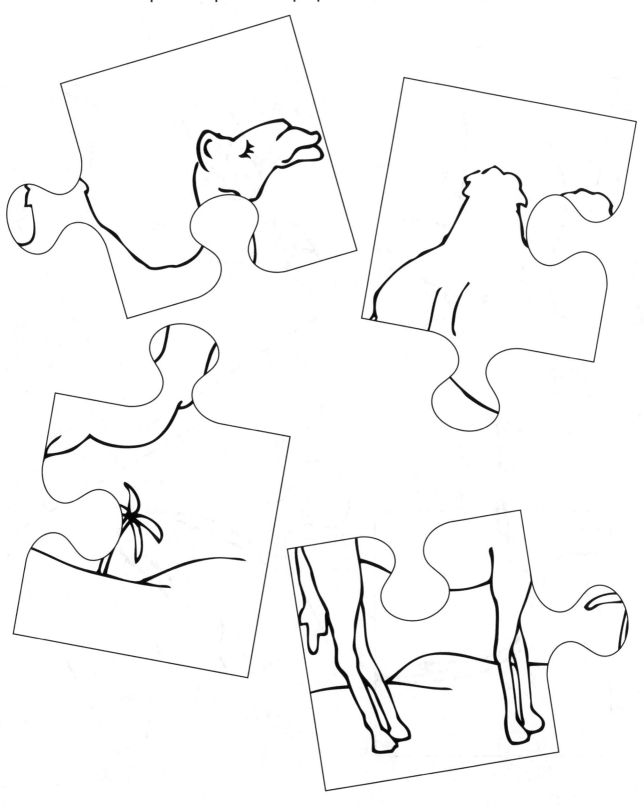

Look at the puzzle pieces. Decide what picture is on the puzzle.
Draw it on a separate piece of paper.

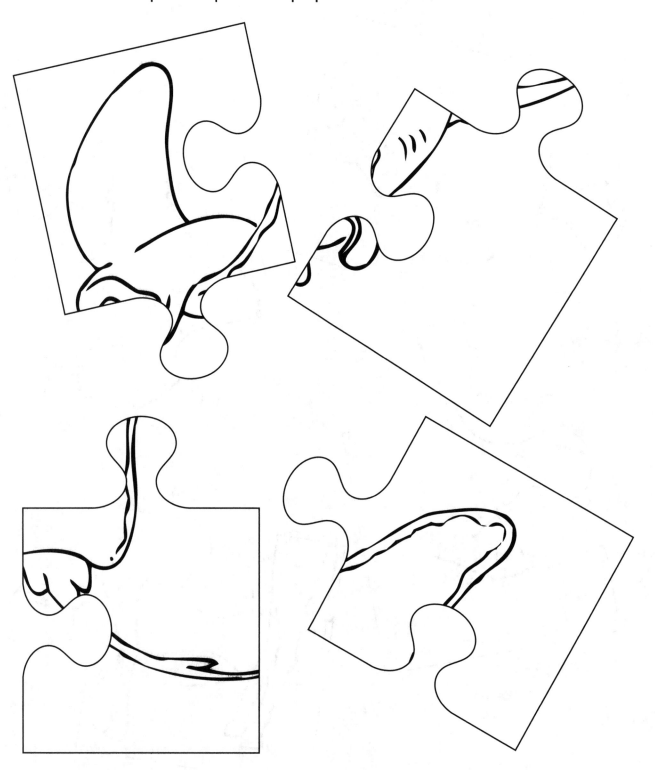

Lesson 46

Draw a line to connect the pictures that go together.

1    **a**

2    **b**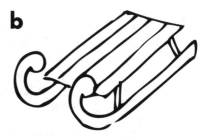

3    **c**

Draw a line to connect the pictures that go together.

1

a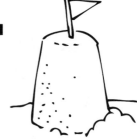

2

b

3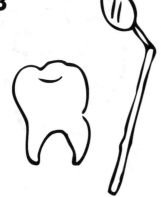

c

Can you guess what these pictures are?

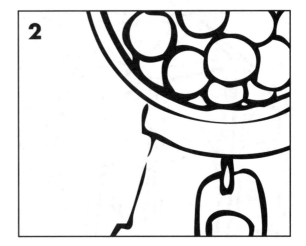

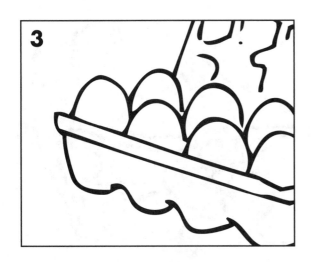

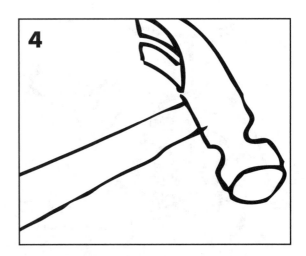

Can you guess what these pictures are?

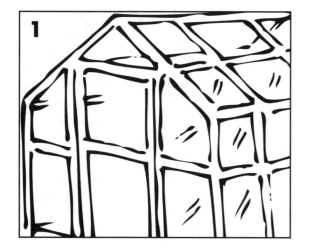

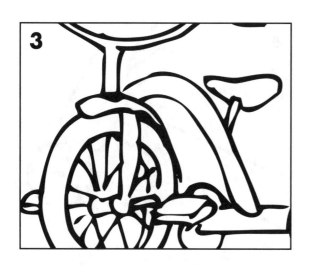

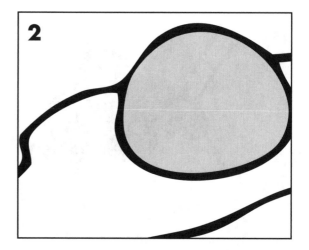

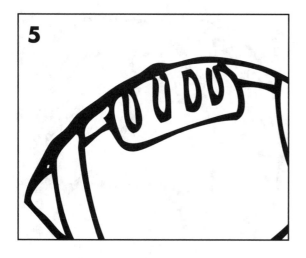

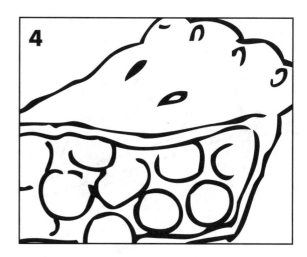

These are leemoys.

These are **not** leemoys.

Draw a **circle** around all of these things that **are** leemoys. Draw an **X through** all of the things that are **not** leemoys.

1

2

3
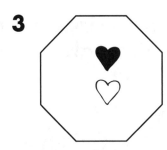

4

5

6
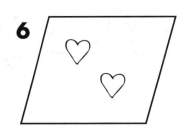

7
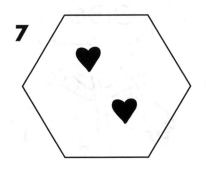

8
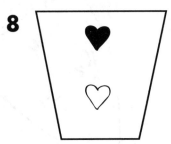

9
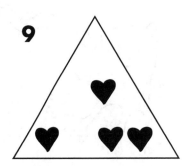

These are shootles.

These are **not** shootles.

Draw a **circle** around all of these things that **are** shootles. Draw an **X through** all of the things that are **not** shootles.

These are beltazoids.

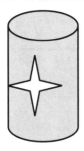  

These are **not** beltazoids.

 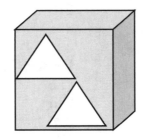 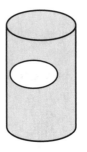

Draw a **circle** around all of these things that **are** beltazoids. Draw an **X through** all of the things that are **not** beltazoids.

1

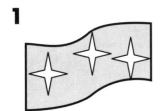

2

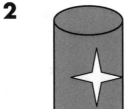

3

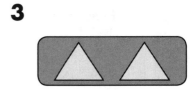

4

5

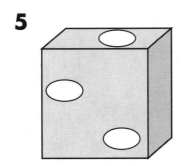

6

Answers

Lesson 1
1. f   4. b
2. c   5. e
3. d   6. a

Lesson 2
1. d   4. a
2. c   5. f
3. b   6. e

Lesson 3
1. a   4. c
2. d   5. e
3. b   6. f

Lesson 4
1. c   4. f
2. a   5. d
3. e   6. b

Lesson 5
1. e   4. d
2. b   5. a
3. c   6. f

Lesson 6
1. c   4. d
2. f   5. e
3. a   6. b

Lesson 7
1. a   4. c
2. f   5. e
3. b   6. d

Lesson 8
1. d   4. e
2. f   5. a
3. c   6. b

Lesson 9
1. c   4. c
2. b   5. a
3. b

Lesson 10
1. b   4. b
2. b   5. b
3. c

Lesson 11
1. b   4. a
2. a   5. a
3. c

Lesson 12
1. b   4. c
2. a   5. a
3. c

Lesson 13
Circle 1, 3, 4, 5, and 7

Lesson 14
Circle 2, 3, 5, 7, 9, and 10

Lesson 15
Circle 2, 3, 5, 6, 8, and 10

Lesson 16
Circle 1, 3, 5, 6, 7, 8, and 10

Lesson 17
1. b   4. b
2. b   5. a
3. c

Lesson 18

1. b	4. b
2. a	5. a
3. c	

Lesson 19

1. b	4. c
2. a	5. b
3. b	

Lesson 20

1. b	3. a
2. c	4. b

Lesson 21

1. c	3. c
2. b	4. c

Lesson 22

1. b	3. c
2. c	4. b

Lesson 23

1. c	3. b
2. c	4. a

Lesson 24

1. b	3. c
2. a	4. a

Lesson 25

Sebastian: Pork Egg Foo Young
Evan: Sesame Chicken
Emma: General Tso's Beef
Falon: Shrimp Fried Rice

Lesson 26

Rob: hummingbird green / red velvet
Tyler: mulberry purple / jack-o-lantern orange
Sydney: swallowtail yellow / cedar green
Lydia: watermelon pink / robin's egg blue

Lesson 27

Nick: string cheese
Clayton: juice pouches
Crystal: strawberry leather
Julie: apple slices

Lesson 28

Grandma Tonia: birds in the salt marshes
Grandpa Dave: former President Bill Clinton
Becky: collecting shells
Sebastian: turtle sanctuary

Lesson 29

Logan: Bouncing Air Arcade
Jackson: Magic Park
Dakota: Water Park
Taylor: Victorian Doll Museum

Lesson 30

Aidan: making lavender cookies
Landon: sampling lemonade and jelly
Chloe: crafting lavender wreaths
Kaitlyn: gathering bundles of lavender

Lesson 31

Colby: going down the giant slide
Adam: putting golf balls
Shannon: eating funnel cake
Tasha: fishing for prizes

Lesson 32
1. c
2. a
3. d
4. e
5. b

Lesson 33
1. e
2. d
3. a
4. b
5. c

Lesson 34
1. c
2. a
3. b
4. e
5. d

Lesson 35
1. a
2. d
3. b
4. e
5. c

Lesson 36
1. d
2. c
3. a
4. b
5. e

Lesson 37
1. d
2. e
3. b
4. c
5. a

Lesson 38
1. c
2. e
3. d
4. a
5. b

Lesson 39
1. d
2. b
3. e
4. a
5. c

Lesson 40
1. b
2. c
3. d
4. a

Lesson 41
1. d
2. c
3. b
4. a

Lesson 42
1. b
2. b
3. a
4. a

Lesson 43
1. a
2. c
3. a
4. b

Lesson 44
camel

Lesson 45
sting ray

Lesson 46
1. b
2. c
3. a

Lesson 47
1. c
2. a
3. b

Lesson 48
1. sundae
2. bubblegum machine
3. egg carton
4. hammer
5. pansy / flower
6. nickel

Lesson 49
1. greenhouse
2. egg
3. tricycle
4. cherry pie
5. football
6. saddle

Lesson 50
Leemoys are unshaded geometric figures with all straight sides enclosing an even number of shaded objects. Circle 2, 4, 7, and 9.

Lesson 51
Shootles are creatures that do **not** have the same number of eyes as they have hands. Circle 2, 4, and 5.

Lesson 52
Beltazoids are figures with one or more stars on them. Circle 1, 2, and 4.

About the Authors

This mother-and-son team has coauthored a number of books, including an initial collaboration on *Lollipop Logic Book 1* in 1990. **Bonnie Risby** has been a classroom teacher of French, English, sixth grade, and gifted education; a family therapist; an author; and a businesswoman. Her books include *Thinking Through Analogies, Orbiting With Logic, Analogies for the 21st Century*, the Connections: Activities for Deductive Thinking series, and the Logic Safari series. **Robert K. Risby, II**, the inspiration for this book, always showed an unusual aptitude for logical thinking and became a published author at the age of 6.

Presently, Rob follows a career while pursuing a business degree, and Bonnie continues working in a family business. Both love sports, movies, float trips down Ozark streams, travel, and spending time with friends and family.